THE HISTORY OF THE **TENNESSEE TITANS**

Published by Creative Education

123 South Broad Street

Mankato, Minnesota 56001

Creative Education is an imprint of The Creative Company.

DESIGN AND PRODUCTION BY **EVANSDAY DESIGN**

LIBRARY OF CONGRESS CATALOGING-IN-PUBLICATION DATA

Frisch, Aaron.

The history of the Tennessee Titans / by Aaron Frisch.

p. cm. — (NFL today)

Summary: Traces the history of the team from its beginnings through 2003.

ISBN 1-58341-316-2

1. Tennessee Titans (Football team)—History—Juvenile literature. 2. Houston Oilers (Football team)—History—Juvenile literature. 3. Tennessee Oilers (Football
team)—History—Juvenile literature. [1. Tennessee Titans (Football team)—History. 2. Houston Oilers (Football team)—History. 3. Tennessee Oilers (Football
team)—History. 4. Football—History.] I. Title. II. Series.

GV956.T45F75 2004

796.332′64′0976819—dc22   2003065039

First edition

9 8 7 6 5 4 3 2 1

COVER PHOTO: quarterback Steve McNair

TITANS

THE STATE OF **TENNESSEE** HAS LONG BEEN ASSOCIATED WITH MUSIC. THE CITY OF MEMPHIS WAS THE HOMETOWN OF FAMOUS SINGER ELVIS PRESLEY AND IS CONSIDERED ONE OF THE BIRTHPLACES OF JAZZ AND BLUES MUSIC. THE CITY OF NASHVILLE, THE STATE'S CAPITAL AND LARGEST CITY, HAS MANY RE-CORDING STUDIOS AND IS REGARDED AS THE COUNTRY MUSIC CAPITAL OF THE WORLD. NASHVILLE IS ALSO KNOWN FOR ITS MANY BUILDINGS OF CLASSICAL GREEK DESIGN AND IS SOMETIMES CALLED THE "ATHENS OF THE SOUTH." SO WHEN TENNESSEE BECAME THE NEW HOME OF A NATIONAL FOOTBALL LEAGUE (NFL) TEAM IN 1997, IT WAS FITTING THAT THE TEAM TOOK ITS IDENTITY FROM GREEK MYTHOLOGY. THE TITANS—A RACE OF GIANTS EVEN MORE POWERFUL THAN THE GODS—SEEMED THE PERFECT NAME, AND THE TENNESSEE TITANS WERE BORN.

[Running back Eddie George]

THE TITANS FRANCHISE started out not on the blue-grass hills of Tennessee, but on the dusty plains of Texas. The team was founded in 1959 by K.S. "Bud" Adams, a wealthy oil businessman and football fan. Adams wanted to build an NFL team in the city of Houston. When the NFL rejected the idea, he built a team anyway as part of a new league called the American Football League (AFL). The team, named the Oilers, was one of eight clubs in the new league.

The Oilers began building their roster by signing speedy running back Billy Cannon, who had just won the Heisman Trophy as the best college football player in America. They then found their quarterback (and kicker) when they brought a 33-year-old NFL veteran named George Blanda out of retirement. The seemingly ageless Blanda would go on to play professional football until he

was 48. "Some quarterbacks…throw the ball about the same way every time," Oakland Raiders safety Dave Grayson once noted. "But not George. You can't read him. One time he'll drill it, the next time he'll loft it a little, then he'll float it."

With Blanda and Cannon leading the offense and cornerback Mark Johnston spurring the defense, the Oilers were a Texas-sized success. In their first season, they went 10–4. In the AFL championship game, 32,000 fans packed into Jeppesen Stadium— a renovated high school field that served as the Oilers' home—to watch Houston beat the Los Angeles Chargers 24–16.

In 1961, Houston started the season just 1–3 but fought back to win its division. With the help of sensational wide receiver Charley Hennigan, the team then fended off the Chargers again in the championship game. A year later, Houston fans almost saw their team "three-peat." The Oilers reached the 1962 AFL title game but came up just short, losing to the Dallas Texans on a field goal in double overtime.

THE OILERS FELL back to earth in 1963, suffering the first of four straight losing seasons. The team made another run at a championship in 1967 after adding speedy safety Ken Houston and rookie linebacker George Webster to a defense that already featured standout tackle Ed Husmann and safety Fred Glick. These players led Houston to within one game of the Super Bowl in 1967 (in those days, the AFL champs played the NFL champs in the Super Bowl). But in the AFL championship game, the Oilers lost to the Oakland Raiders, 40–7.

In 1968, the Oilers added another star: defensive lineman Elvin Bethea. With a frightening combination of quickness and power, Bethea quickly gave the Oilers a fearsome pass rush. The one-man wrecking crew would play 16 seasons and 210 games for the Oilers, more than any other player in franchise history. "The [thing] about Elvin," Bethea's college coach Hornsby Howell later explained, "was that he was the kind of athlete who worked hard even when nobody was watching him."

With Blanda, Houston, and Bethea (all eventual Hall-of-Famers) wearing Oilers blue, Houston fans saw some good shows throughout the '60s. Yet from 1963 to 1970, the team enjoyed just one winning season. Houston continued to struggle even after adding talented quarterback Dan Pastorini with the first overall pick in the 1971 NFL Draft (the Oilers had joined the NFL when the two leagues merged into one in 1970). In both 1972 and 1973, the Oilers went just 1–13.

IN 1975, THE OILERS made a coaching change, promoting defensive coordinator O.A. "Bum" Phillips to head coach. Phillips was a colorful character who often paced the sidelines in a 10-gallon hat, snakeskin boots, and a plaid Western shirt. He quickly assembled a defense that included Bethea and linebackers Gregg Bingham and Robert Brazile. On offense, he gave Pastorini two great passing targets in receivers Ken Burrough and Billy "White Shoes" Johnson.

The Oilers went 10–4 in 1975, their first winning season in eight years. One of the big stories that season was the play of Johnson, who tied an NFL record by returning four kicks for touchdowns. Known for his bright white shoes and goofy end zone dances, the 5-foot-9 Johnson was a marvel to watch as he darted away from his much larger opponents. "He was even more exciting in practice," Phillips recalled. "We didn't have anyone who could tackle him."

Relentless linebacker Gregg Bingham was the Oilers' leading tackler every year from 1974 to 1981^

The 1975 season was a good one, but it wasn't until 1978 that Houston really emerged as an American Football Conference (AFC) powerhouse. That year, the Oilers drafted Earl Campbell, a 230-pound running back from the nearby University of Texas. Combining great speed, incredible strength, and a bit of nastiness, Campbell soon became one of the NFL's most feared runners.

Campbell enjoyed punishing would-be tacklers and always seemed to veer into defenders instead of away from them. This bruising style was showcased during a nationally televised Monday night game his rookie season. In that game, Campbell ran over and around the Miami Dolphins for 199 yards and four touchdowns. Defenders throughout the NFL quickly came to respect his power; as Dallas Cowboys end John Dutton explained, "I just tried to grab him and hold on for dear life until help arrived."

The Oilers reached the AFC championship game in both 1978 and 1979. Unfortunately, they lost both times to the Pittsburgh Steelers and their "Steel Curtain" defense. In 1980, Campbell rushed for almost 2,000 yards, but the Oilers were bounced from the playoffs again. After that loss, Phillips was fired as head coach.

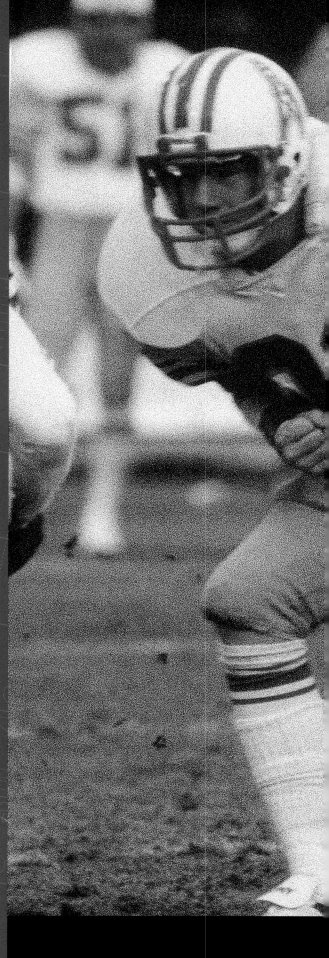

A fast and physical defense has been a team trademark since the days of Elvin Bethea and Robert Brazile.

IN THE EARLY 1980s, the Oilers went through several coaches and became one of the worst teams in the NFL. Bethea, Johnson, and many other stars of the '70s either left town or retired, and Campbell was slowed by increasingly bad knees. In 1983, the Oilers went just 2–14.

Houston's decline was finally stopped in 1985, when assistant coach Jerry Glanville took over as head coach. To return Houston to glory, Glanville wanted to turn the Astrodome—an indoor stadium that had served as the team's home since 1968—into a "House of Pain" for opponents. To do this, he set out to make his team more aggressive and physical. "When I came here in '84, we had the nicest guys in the NFL," Glanville later joked. "But they couldn't hit if you handed them sticks."

Cornerback Cris Dishman used his size and speed to shut down opposing teams' top passing targets

Ernest Givins made a club-record 542 career catches ^

Haywood Jeffires played in the Pro Bowl three times ^

Glanville built up his defense by adding swift cornerback Cris Dishman and linemen Ray Childress and William Fuller. The new coach built his offense around quarterback Warren Moon, who had arrived in Houston in 1984 after spending six seasons with the Edmonton Eskimos, a team in the Canadian Football League (CFL). The strong-armed Moon had dominated the competition in Canada, leading his team to the CFL championship five years in a row. In Houston, he was soon firing passes to talented receivers Drew Hill, Ernest Givins, and Haywood Jeffires.

With fans showing up at the Astrodome in record numbers, the Oilers went 9–6 in 1987 and made the playoffs for the first of seven straight seasons. However, getting to the playoffs was one thing; getting to the Super Bowl was another. After Houston lost in the playoffs in 1987, 1988, and 1989, Glanville was fired and replaced by former NFL linebacker Jack Pardee.

Coach Pardee quickly made an offensive change. Relying on Moon's scrambling ability and quick throwing release, he designed plays in which the quarterback would roll toward the sidelines and fire passes to receivers streaking across or down the field—an offense that became known as the "Run-and-Shoot." In 1990 and 1991, Moon was sensational, passing for almost 4,700 yards each season.

Unfortunately, the Oilers continued to struggle in the postseason. Losses in 1990 and 1991 were painful, but the most heartbreaking playoff game of all took place after the 1992 season. The 10–6 Oilers traveled to Buffalo in the first round of the playoffs and came out swinging, battering the Bills and running up a 35–3 lead by early in the third quarter. But combining quick-strike touchdown passes with daring onside kickoffs, Buffalo staged the greatest comeback in NFL playoff history to tie the game 38–38 and force overtime. Minutes later, the Bills booted a field goal to seal Houston's collapse.

A receiver with a knack for finding holes in opposing defenses, Drew Hill was a valuable offensive threat.

BY 1994, MOON and Pardee were gone, and former assistant Jeff Fisher had been named head coach. Fisher quickly rebuilt the team, drafting quarterback Steve McNair in 1995 and running back Eddie George in 1996. McNair was a tough and athletic passer who had earned the nickname "Air McNair" in college for his exciting style of play. George was a big (6-foot-3 and 230 pounds) and powerful runner who had just won the Heisman Trophy. Together, the duo would become the heart of the team's offense for the next decade.

For several years, Bud Adams had wanted the city of Houston to help build a new football stadium. The city did not support the idea, so in 1997, Adams moved the Oilers to Tennessee. The team put together two mediocre seasons playing in a stadium in Memphis, but in 1999, a new era began as the team moved into the beautiful new Adelphia Coliseum in Nashville. It took the field as the

Tennessee Titans, having changed its name, uniform, and logo before the season. Adding to the excitement level was the team's top pick in the 1999 NFL Draft: defensive end Jevon Kearse.

Kearse was a physical marvel. Standing 6-foot-4 and weighing 260 pounds, he had huge hands and long arms. He also had the speed of a wide receiver, the vertical leap of a pro basketball player, and a nonstop motor—all of which had earned him the nickname "the Freak" during his college days at the University of Florida. Kearse's skills left opponents in awe. "You think you've got him blocked, and the ball is in the air, and all of a sudden he's downfield making the tackle or stripping the ball," said Pittsburgh Steelers offensive coordinator Kevin Gilbride.

Kearse lived up to the hype, setting an NFL rookie record with 14.5 quarterback sacks in 1999. And with McNair directing the offense, George rushing for more than 1,000 yards for the fourth straight season, and safety Blaine Bishop and cornerback Samari Rolle leading a tough defense, the Titans soared to a 13–3 record.

Tennessee's amazing season got even better in the playoffs. In a first-round matchup against Buffalo, Bills players began celebrating their victory after scoring with three seconds left to take a 16–15 lead. But on the ensuing kickoff, Titans tight end

Kevin Carter made 10 quarterback sacks in 2002 ^

Tight end Frank Wycheck was a clutch receiver ^

Frank Wycheck carried the ball to the right, then threw it across the field to receiver Kevin Dyson, who followed a wall of blockers to the end zone as Tennessee fans went crazy in the stands. Energized by the "Music City Miracle," as the incredible play became known, the Titans then advanced to the Super Bowl. Tennessee could not drum up another miracle, however, losing 23–16 to the St. Louis Rams in a thrilling contest.

The Titans remained an elite team in the seasons that followed. With the help of such additions as defensive end Kevin Carter, Tennessee went 13–3 in 2000, 11–5 in 2002, and 12–4 in 2003. Although the Titans came up short of a return trip to the Super Bowl all three times, their fans remained hopeful. With an offense in the hands of George, McNair, and wide receiver Derrick Mason, and a defense anchored by linebacker Keith Bulluck, the Titans were poised to wreak havoc in the new AFC South Division in 2004 and beyond.

The story of the Titans franchise is a rich one that spans two leagues and five decades. Having captured two AFL titles in their days as the Oilers and one AFC championship in their Tennessee years, the Titans have stood tall throughout their history. Today's Titans hope to soon add a Super Bowl victory to this history and give the "Music City" something to sing about.

INDEX>